POCAHONTAS

Bridging Two Worlds

AMERICAN HEROES

Pocahontas

Bridging Two Worlds

LARRY DANE BRIMNER

Marshall Cavendish
Benchmark
New York

For my young friends at Menlo Park Elementary in Tucson, Arizona

Marshall Cavendish Benchmark
99 White Plains Road
Tarrytown, New York 10591
www.marshallcavendish.us

Library of Congress Cataloging-in-Publication Data
Brimner, Larry Dane.
Pocahontas : bridging two worlds / by Larry Dane Brimner.
p. cm. — (American heroes)
Summary: "A juvenile biography of the famous Native American woman who helped the Jamestown settlers"—Provided by publisher.
Includes bibliographical references and index.
ISBN 978-0-7614-3065-0
1. Pocahontas, d. 1617—Juvenile literature. 2. Powhatan Indians—Biography—Juvenile literature. 3. Jamestown (Va.)—History—Juvenile literature. I. Title.
E99.P85P5718 2009
975.5′01092—dc22
[B]
2008014411

Editor: Joyce Stanton   Art Director: Anahid Hamparian
Publisher: Michelle Bisson   Designer: Anne Scatto

135642
Printed in Malaysia

Images provided by Debbie Needleman, Picture Researcher, Portsmouth, NH. from the following sources:
Front cover: Pocahontas, 1616 (oil on canvas) by English School. ©Private Collection/Peter Newark American Pictures/The Bridgeman Art Library.
Back cover: MPI/Hulton Archive/Getty Images.
Page i: Pocahontas, 1616 (oil on canvas) by English School. Private Collection/Peter Newark American Picture/The Bridgeman Art Library;
page ii: The Library of Virginia; *page vi:* Three Lions/Hulton Archive/Getty Images;
page 3: The New York Public Library/Art Resource, NY;
pages 4,29: Hulton Archive/Getty Images;
pages 7,18: MPI/Hulton Archive/Getty Images;
page 8: English School/The Bridgeman Art Library/Getty Images; *page 10:* ©British Museum/Art Resource, NY; *page 13:* Pocahontas Saving the Life of Captain John Smith, c. 1836–40, (oil on canvas) by John Gadsby Chapman (1808-09), ©Collection of the New York Historical Society, USA/The Bridgeman Art Library; *page 15:* Archive Photos/Hulton Archive/Getty Images; *pages 17, 23, 27:* The Granger Collection, New York; *page 20:* Copyright 1996, Virginia Historical Society, Richmond, Virginia; *page 25:* The Jamestown–Yorktown Foundation; *page 30:* The Borough of King's Lynn and West Norfolk; *pages 33, 34:* ©Nancy Carter/North Wind Picture Archives; *page 40:* North Wind Picture Archives

CONTENTS

Pocahontas was a Native-American princess. She and her people lived in the Chesapeake Bay area of Virginia.

Pocahontas

Pocahontas was a Native-American princess. Her real name was Matoaka, but the people who knew her called her by her nickname. Pocahontas means "playful little girl" in the language of her people, and Pocahontas *was* playful and spirited. She was also curious and friendly. She helped the English who had come to start a settlement in what is now the Chesapeake Bay area of Virginia.

Pocahontas was born around 1595. This was long before the United States was a country. Her father was Chief Powhatan. He was a powerful leader who ruled an empire of about twenty-eight tribes. The Powhatans hunted, farmed the land, and fished the waters.

In December of 1606, the English set sail across the Atlantic Ocean to look for gold and a shorter water route to the Pacific Ocean. The expedition landed in America on May 14, 1607, and immediately started building a fort on a river close to many Powhatan villages. They named the river after their king, King James. They called the settlement Jamestown.

The Powhatans lived in small villages like this one.
They hunted, farmed, and fished.

Soon after landing, the settlers began building Jamestown, a fort named after England's King James I.

Life was difficult for the Jamestown settlers. During the voyage, strong winds had delayed them and they had used up much of their food supplies. Then, not long after landing, they were attacked by a band of unfriendly Native Americans. Adding to these difficulties, some of the settlers were noblemen who did not like to work. Captain John Smith, one of Jamestown's leaders, couldn't understand their laziness. He said they "would rather starve and rot" than feed themselves. Instead of planting crops, these noblemen put their hopes in a supply ship that was scheduled to reach Jamestown in November.

Unfortunately, the schedules of sailing vessels were never certain. November came and went. The promised supplies did not arrive, so the settlers sought help from their Indian neighbors. They traded copper utensils and beads, glass trinkets, and iron hatchets for corn, fish, oysters, and bread. In this way, they collected enough food to survive for the moment.

The settlers traded with their Indian neighbors for food.

Captain John Smith, one of the leaders of Jamestown

With food in the storehouse, Captain Smith turned to other business, namely finding a shortcut to the Pacific Ocean. He had no idea how far away it was. He set out in early December to explore the James River and its tributaries. Would one of them be a route across the American continent? Some fifty miles up the Chickahominy River, Smith and his men stopped to rest and eat. During the break, they were attacked by a band of Powhatans and all of Smith's men were killed. Smith was captured and turned over to Chief Powhatan. This chief of chiefs would decide Captain Smith's fate.

*Guards, perhaps wearing body paint like this man,
brought Captain Smith before Chief Powhatan.*

Held by guards, Captain Smith stood before Chief Powhatan. Nearby, men with clubs in their hands waited. At the chief's side, a girl around twelve or thirteen years of age looked on. The girl was Chief Powhatan's "dearest daughter," Pocahontas.

Chief Powhatan made his decision. Two large stones were placed before him. Captain Smith was made to kneel with his head upon the stones. The men with clubs moved forward.

Just then, Pocahontas rushed over to Captain Smith. She laid her head upon his, as Captain Smith later told the story, to save him from death.

Seeing this, Chief Powhatan changed his mind. Captain Smith might live, but only to make hatchets for Chief Powhatan and beads and bells for Pocahontas.

Nobody knows if Captain Smith's story about Pocahontas is true. Captain Smith didn't write about Pocahontas until many years later. A lot of people suspect that he made things up to make his capture more interesting. Other people are less suspicious and believe that Pocahontas really did perform such a brave act.

Pocahontas's brave act saved Captain Smith's life.

Captain Smith remained a prisoner for two days more. Then Chief Powhatan freed him and said that they were friends. He gave him permission to return to Jamestown and told him to send back "two great guns, and a grindstone."

Captain Smith did not trust the chief, so he tricked the guides who were sent with him to Jamestown. He offered them two guns and a grindstone, but they were too heavy for the men to carry. They accepted instead only a few small trinkets.

*Trinkets such as carved wooden dolls appealed to the
Native Americans, who had never seen things
quite like them before.*

After that, Pocahontas visited Captain Smith and the English settlers often. She played games with the boys. She brought food for the struggling people. Without her help, Captain Smith said, they would have "starved with hunger."

Pocahontas continued her visits, once every four or five days, for many months. Then, on a visit in 1609, she heard some sad news. The settlers told her that Captain Smith had died. Upon hearing this, she stopped coming to Jamestown. In truth, Captain Smith had been hurt in a hunting accident and had been sent back to England.

Pocahontas visited Jamestown often, bringing food to the struggling settlers.

Chief Powhatan was unhappy when more settlers came to Jamestown.
He tried to drive them away.

By now, more settlers had arrived in Jamestown. Chief Powhatan feared that his people would lose their lands to the English. He decided to starve Jamestown out of existence. He captured settlers. He took guns.

The people in Jamestown were desperate. They had so little food that they were eating dogs, cats, and even their old boots and shoes. But Samuel Argall, captain of a supply ship, had a plan.

Captain Argall got Pocahontas to board his ship, and then held her captive.

Captain Argall tricked Pocahontas into boarding his ship and held her captive. He sent word to Chief Powhatan that he would trade her for the captured settlers and guns—and food. Chief Powhatan released the settlers, but he wasn't interested in the rest of the deal. Pocahontas remained a captive.

Pocahontas was angry with the settlers. She had shown them friendship in earlier times. Now she was their prisoner, although they treated her kindly.

During her captivity, the settlers taught her English manners. They dressed her in English clothes. They taught her to be a Christian and gave her a new name: Rebecca.

During her captivity, Pocahontas learned English ways
and became a Christian.

Pocahontas was also angry with her father. He had placed more value on guns than on his daughter.

When Pocahontas was returned to Chief Powhatan almost a year later, she refused to stay with him. She had grown accustomed to her new life. And while she was a captive, she had met a tobacco farmer named John Rolfe. They had fallen in love and wished to marry.

Chief Powhatan agreed to the marriage. He made peace with the settlers. This was called the Peace of Pocahontas, and it lasted eight years.

John Rolfe, a tobacco farmer, fell in love
with Pocahontas and wanted to marry her.

Pocahontas and John Rolfe were married on April 5, 1614. About a year later, they had a son. They named him Thomas.

A few months later, Jamestown's leaders devised a plan to help the colony. They would send John Rolfe to England, accompanied by his Native-American bride and baby son. They hoped the family would spark new interest in the colony and that more English people would want to invest money in it and settle there.

Pocahontas and John Rolfe were wed on April 5, 1614.

Pocahontas liked England, and the English people liked her. She was quite a celebrity. She was even presented to the king. Then, something unexpected happened. Pocahontas received a visit from an old friend. It was none other than Captain John Smith!

It was an uncomfortable reunion, though, for both of them. Pocahontas had, after all, believed that he was dead. She was angry that he hadn't visited sooner, especially since she had shown him such friendship back in America.

It was to be their last meeting.

In England, Pocahontas was a celebrity. Everyone wanted to meet her. She even had her portrait painted.

Pocahontas and her son, Thomas,
shortly before they set sail for home

In March 1617, Pocahontas set sail for Virginia with John and Thomas. She had not been feeling well, however. London's polluted air had made her ill. The ship had only gone a short distance before she felt too sick to travel. The captain dropped anchor near Gravesend, England, and Pocahontas was taken ashore. She died there on March 21 and was buried the same day.

John Rolfe continued on to Virginia, where he became a successful tobacco farmer. Two-year-old Thomas was raised in England by Rolfe's brother. At the age of twenty, Thomas returned to Virginia and his father's tobacco farm.

In her short life, Pocahontas played an important role in American history. She wasn't afraid to reach out to strangers who were in need. On her own, she built a bridge between two very different worlds. The compassion and generosity she showed to America's early settlers will always be remembered.

Pocahontas bridged two worlds. Because of this,
she is remembered as a peacemaker.

IMPORTANT DATES

1595 The likely date that Pocahontas was born, although no one is really certain.

1606 December 19 and 20, members of the first Jamestown voyage board the *Susan Constant*, the *Godspeed*, and the *Discovery*.

1607 The *Susan Constant*, the *Godspeed*, and the *Discovery* reach North America on May 14.

The site for Jamestown is chosen.

Captain John Smith is captured in December and Pocahontas saves his life.

1609 Pocahontas is told that Captain John Smith is dead.

1613 Captain Samuel Argall tricks Pocahontas into boarding his ship, and she is held captive.

1614 Pocahontas decides to remain with the English.

She and John Rolfe, a tobacco farmer, marry on April 5.

1615 Thomas Rolfe is born.

1616 Pocahontas, called Lady Rebecca by the English, arrives in London.

1617 Pocahontas dies March 21 and is buried the same day in Gravesend, England.

WORDS TO KNOW

band A group of people.

compassion Caring or feeling sympathy for someone struck by hardship.

continent One of the large areas of land that make up the globe.

English A person or persons from England.

expedition A group of people making a journey for a particular purpose.

grindstone A stone wheel used for sharpening knives and hatchets; also a stone for grinding corn and other grains.

Native Americans American Indians; the first people to live in North America.

noblemen Men born into wealthy and high-ranking families.

settlers People who move into a new land.

tributaries Streams and rivers that flow into a larger river.

trinkets Small objects or pieces of jewelry that have little value.

utensils Small articles such as bowls and plates.

To Learn More about Pocahontas

WEB SITES

Jamestown Rediscovery
http://www.apva.org/jr.html

Kid Info
http://www.kidinfo.com/American_History/
Colonization_Jamestown.html

The Library of Congress Presents America's Story from America's Library
http://www.americaslibrary.gov/cgi-bin/page.cgi

Spectrum Home & School Network
http://www.incwell.com/Biographies/Pocahontas.html

BOOKS

In Their Own Words: Pocahontas by George Sullivan. Scholastic, 2002.

Pocahontas by Lucia Raatma, Compass Point Books. 2001.

Pocahontas and the Strangers by Clyde Robert Bulla. Scholastic Paperbacks, 1988.

Pocahontas: Princess of the New World by Kathleen Krull. Walker Books for Young Readers, 2007.

PLACES TO VISIT

Historic Jamestowne
1368 Colonial Parkway
Jamestown, VA 23081
PHONE: (757) 229-1733
WEB SITE: **http://www.nps.gov/jame/**

Jamestown Settlement / Yorktown Victory Center
2218 Jamestown Road
Route 31 S.
Williamsburg, VA 23185
PHONE: (757) 253-4838
WEB SITE: **http://www.historyisfun.org**

INDEX

Page numbers for illustrations are in boldface.

A Note on Quotes

What we know about the legend of Pocahontas comes from *The Generall Historie of Virginia, New-England, and the Summer Isles: with the Names of the Adventurers, Planters, and Governours from Their First Beginning Ano: 1584 to This Present 1624.* This was Captain John Smith's major book. In earlier writings, he had failed to report his rescue from death by Pocahontas. Because the details of his rescue weren't written until after Pocahontas had become a celebrity in England

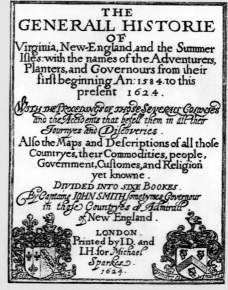

and died there, many researchers cast doubt on whether the events happened as he reported. Whether it is fact or fiction, the legend of Pocahontas is one of the most often told tales in American history. The quotations used in this book come from a reprint edition of Smith's book.

ABOUT THE AUTHOR

LARRY DANE BRIMNER is the author of almost 150 books for children, many of them award-winners. Among his fiction and nonfiction titles are *A Migrant Family*, an NCSS/CBC Notable Trade Book in the Field of Social Studies; *The Littlest Wolf*, an IRA/CBC Children's Choice book, an Oppenheim Gold Medal recipient, and a 2004 Great Lakes' Great Books (Michigan) Honor book; and *Subway: The Story of Tunnels, Tubes, and Tracks*, a Junior Library Guild selection. Larry makes his home in Tucson, Arizona. To learn more about him, investigate his Web site at www.brimner.com.